"In the many years that I have been privileged to preach across America, Africa, Europe, Asia, the South Pacific and the Caribbean I have observed one common ingredient in the heart of every successful pastor both in America and worldwide: Each highly successful pastor has demonstrated a burning passion for the winning of the souls of those who are lost. An unquenchable evangelistic fervor is the priceless ingredient in ministry success!

"Dr. Angelo Quinlan, as a seasoned and proven bishop and pastor of the Lord's church has years of experience and success in reaching out effectively to the lost! I am glad that the Holy Spirit has commissioned him to write this book which shares the wisdom of his heart, life and ministry. The contents of this book will add to your evangelistic arsenal and will expose you and those under your influence to concepts, principles and techniques which will enhance your ability to participate in reaping the great spiritual harvest destined for these last days. The hour is late! The Lord is soon to come! The issue is urgent! I am pleased to heartily endorse this book and this author."

—Apostle Henry B. Alexander
Pastor and founder of the Shield of Faith Christian Center and the founder and Presiding Apostle of the Shield of Faith Fellowship of Churches, International, Inc.

"The role of the American ambassador to Russia is to represent America in Russia. Even so the Christian ambassador is to represent Heaven on Earth. The lifestyle of the ambassador is to demonstrate how to live on Earth. The residence of the ambassador is called the embassy—it is Heaven's property on Earth. While in a foreign country the ambassador lives under diplomat immunity. Diplomatic immunity is a form of legal immunity that ensures diplomats are given safe passage and are considered not susceptible to lawsuit or prosecution under the host country's laws. When a person wants to defect from his own country he must make his way to the embassy. It is the role of the ambassador to grant asylum to the defector. In the custody of the ambassador the defector is protected from his own nation. Under the rules of diplomatic immunity the ambassador is free to travel without restriction.

As ambassadors of the gospel our mission is to go into all the world and preach to every creature. Every Christian Ambassador has diplomatic immunity and is not subject to any government on Earth. **This new outreach program called The Kingdom Ambassadors is the fulfillment of the gospel for this generation."**

—BISHOP GREGORY W. NEWMAN
PASTOR OF EL BETHEL IN PHOENIX, AZ AND THE
DIOCESAN OF THE MOUNTAIN STATES COUNCIL

"Pastor Angelo Quinlan is a tremendous speaker, and didactic teacher. Thank you for this very timely and relevant book concerning our role as **Christian Ambassadors**.

"One thing I feel that has negatively affected the growth of True Christianity and the Kingdom of God is that too many of our Christian Ambassadors are functioning as citizens of this world, thereby minimizing at best, even neutralizing their office as Ambassadors through secularized Christianity.

"This book is a must-read for every Christian, and should be a part of your library. I strongly recommend the use of this book as a part of your new members or Christian orientation class. Pastor Quinlan, please continue to publish material of this nature."

—BISHOP JEFFERY D. GOLDSMITH,
DIOCESAN BISHOP OF THE OKLAHOMA STATE COUNCIL
26TH EPISCOPAL DISTRICT OF THE PENTECOSTAL ASSEMBLIES OF THE WORLD, INC.

Kingdom Ambassadors

God's Evangelistic Soul Winning System

Angelo E. Quinlan

New Harvest Time
PUBLICATIONS

Published by New Harvest Time Publications

Copyright © 2017 Angelo E. Quinlan
All rights reserved. No part of this book may
be reproduced, stored, or transmitted by any
means—whether auditory, graphic, mechanical, or
electronic—without written permission of both publisher
and author, except in the case of brief excerpts used in
critical articles and reviews. Unauthorized reproduction
of any part of this work is illegal
and is punishable by law.

ISBN: 978-0-9991777-1-6 (Paperback)

Printed in the U.S.A.

Book Design by DesignForBooks.com

Dedication

Tremendous gratitude I give to the Lord for my Pastor, Bishop J. Grant Tolbert and 1st Lady Delores Tolbert for being extensive mentors to my wife and I as Christian life style mentors. I also give superior thanks to the Lord for my beautiful wife of 42 years. The favor bestowed upon me by the Lord, to have her as the wife of my youth and the mother of my three sons. She has been my friend, my lover, and The Lord's master instrument in my personal life helping with sculpturing relationships. Being her husband has assisted in the development of the man of God and the Ambassador of Christ that I am today.

Thanks also to the membership of New Harvest Time Apostolic Ministries whom I have been privilege to be God's instrument in the development of his people as their pastor for Kingdom business in the earth to his glory.

Contents

1. Networking Evangelistic Team   1
2. The New Creatures in Christ   9
3. Signs of Your Newness   13
4. When Will This Battle Cease?   21
5. The Necessity of the Promise   31
6. Establishing New Believer's Habits   43
7. God's Ammunition against the Kingdom of Darkness   53
8. Your Damascus Road   69
9. The Ministry of Reconciliation   75
10. Your Real Story   87
11. The Witness   89
12. Remembering You Were Forgiven   95
13. Your Kingdom Ambassador Credentials   99
14. Learning to Stay Reconciled   105
15. We Are Christ's Workmanship   115

CHAPTER

Networking Evangelistic Team

The Soul Saving Explosion of the Last Days

God's master plan to touch the sin-sick, trapped world by the preaching of the gospel in the last days is revealed in the scriptures. God revealed the soul-winning system he created to win the world, sharing only with the participants of his divine plan of salvation. The awesomeness of the plan is hidden to the world. Many new believers are void of understanding concerning their purpose or part in God's big picture of salvation. The divine plan is concealed in the word of God, and yet hidden from the wisdom of the unregenerate men. The plan is preserved for those called into the Kingdom of Christ, born again and Spirit filled.

God has the Old Testament prophet Isaiah declare how understanding and revelation will be obtained:

> Who is it he is trying to teach? To whom is he explaining his message? To children weaned from their milk, to those just taken from the breast? For it is: Do this, do that, a rule for this, a rule for that; a little here, a little there. Very well then, with foreign lips and strange tongues God will speak to this people, to whom he said, "This is the resting place, let the weary rest"; and, "This is the place of repose"— but they would not listen. (Isaiah 28:9–12 KJV)

Then in the New Testament, the apostle Paul says:

> But as it is written, eye hath not seen, nor ear heard, neither have entered into the heart of man, the things which God hath prepared for them that love him. But God hath revealed them unto us by his Spirit: for the Spirit searcheth all things, yea, the deep things of God. For what man knoweth the things of a man, save the spirit of man

which is in him? Even so the things of God knoweth no man, but the Spirit of God. (1 Corinthians 2:9–11 KJV)

From the fall of Adam in the garden, God declared that he would reinstate his relationship with mankind to himself with a promise seed.

> **Kingdom Thinking is Imperative for Biblical Understanding**

The apostle Paul writes in the letter to the church in Ephesus concerning the divine structures, purpose, and objective of God's leadership plan for the Kingdom of Christ:

> He gave some, apostles; and some, prophets; and some, evangelists; and some, pastors and teachers; then he reveals why God gave these; For the perfecting of the saints, for the work of the ministry, for the edifying of the body of Christ. (Ephesians 4:11–12 KJV)

God gave apostles, prophets, evangelists, preachers, and teachers for the preparation of the saints of God to work together with him to win the world. Apostle Paul is showing how the Kingdom system works, reminding every unit of its part.

> The mind of Christ is mandatory to understand the objective of Christ

Often the question of new believers is, "What am I to do?" You are those who will be trained through the teaching of the apostles, prophets, evangelists, pastors, and teachers. You are the new ones in the body of Christ.

> If any man be in Christ, he is a new creature: old things are passed away; behold, all things are become new. And all things are of God, who hath reconciled us to himself by Jesus Christ, and hath given to us the ministry of reconciliation. (2 Corinthians 5:17–18 KJV)

Therefore those who are trained have a powerful ministry in the body of Christ. This networking divine system is the greatest and most powerful plan in the Kingdom of God; by divine design you are the ambassadors, the entry-level of every new believer born again in the body of Christ (2 Corinthians 5:20 KJV). These are they who fill the sanctuaries every Sunday in quest of the will of God for their Kingdom assignments on the earth for their lives. The Sunday gatherings and Bible classes are to build faith and serve as reminders of purpose, calling, and personal assignments. This book will disclose empowering information concerning relationships with Christ; enriching relationships with pastors, brothers, and sisters. This book will make plain your divine calling and your personal ministry as a Saint of God.

The application of this information will assist in the development of the mindset necessary to cultivate personal relationships with Christ. This material will also reinforce networking soul-winning strategies within this Kingdom system for evangelizing cities and communities. Your desire to express your gratitude to the Lord for saving you should create a hunger and thirst in you to know more about your new life in Christ Jesus. This deep-down drive within you will be used greatly by spirit within you to guide you to the supporting scriptures in the Bible that pertain to your new walk with Christ. You will be enlightened to the reasons Jesus called you into the Kingdom of God. I recommend that the daily reading of the Bible should begin with your praying for the Spirit to help you clearly understand what is being said. The prayer for you is that this book will cause you to seek the Lord with an expectation of more understanding of what he is requiring of you in his master plan on the earth, opening your understanding and causing hidden revelations written in his word to rise off the pages. The prayer for you is that there will be enlightening revelations. The subject foundational scriptures for these teachings will be established from both Ephesians 4:11–16 and 2 Corinthians 5:17–20, from one of the Pauline epistles.

Apostle Paul is the writer of thirteen New Testament letters to the body of Christ. The writings of Paul will be the guide to navigate us through this lesson concerning the entry-level of ministry of every new believer born again in Christ, your divine assignment as part of the Networking Evangelist Team in the body of Christ. The foundation of the teachings concerning the operation and purpose of this divine system will be taken from both Ephesians 4:11–16 and 2 Corinthians 5:17–20. This is the first level of ministry that God bestows upon every child of God after his bornagain experience of being filled with the Holy Spirit (Romans 8:9). Some may call it the Holy Ghost (Acts 2:3–4), others the promise of the Father (Acts 1:4–5), and there are references to it as living water; all are referring to the same Spirit of Christ within you.

The Body of Christ Networking System

... the whole body fitly joined together and compacted by that which every joint supplieth, according to the effectual working in the measure of every part, maketh increase of the body unto the edifying of itself in love. (Ephesians 4:16 KJV)

> **NOTE:** There will be times that I will only place the scripture chapter and verse in the reading, and other times I will place the whole scripture. As new believers, it is good to search your Bibles to become familiar with book and scripture locations, but at times, to keep the flow of the lesson, I will include the total scripture.

The Parable of the Networking Evangelistic Team

Jesus was always using parables to teach Kingdom principles comparing a natural concept to give understanding to a spiritual teaching. The many Network Marketing Systems have become one of the small business working models of the day. This working business system is two or more moving parts. In actuality, these Network Marketing Business Systems are individuals working together in concert with each other. The lesson to understand is that these systems are biblically based. "Whom the whole body fitly joined together and compacted by that which every joint supplieth, according to the effectual working in the measure of every part, maketh increase of the body unto the edifying of itself in love (Ephesians 4:16 KJV). The success must first have a product that benefits everyone's life and that everyone must think is necessary, although they don't realize it because they don't know what the product does. So the Network Marketing Team has to recruit people, and they have to advertise how marvelous this product is and the benefits it provides.

The Kingdom's product is salvation, the gospel of Jesus Christ. To keep the new recruits educated and encouraged there are weekly rallies when the whole team gathers along with the new recruits. These meetings are opportunities for the members of the team to give progress reports, introduce new recruits, and hear testimonies. The Kingdom of Christ has fellowship gatherings, church services, and Bible studies, to learn, worship, and praise, including daily prayer for thanksgivings and preparation thanking the Lord for his favor, goodness, direction, and mercies. The expectation is that souls will give their lives to Christ daily. The world's expectation is that consumers will become sold on how marvelous the product is, sharing with others. The hope is to recruit consumers daily to become recruiters.

CHAPTER

The New Creatures in Christ

If any man be in Christ, he is a new creature: old things are passed away; behold, all things are become new.

Your new life took place when you repented of your old way of living and the Lord gave you the power of the Holy Ghost. Yes! You are now a new creature in Christ. No longer do you have the desire to live that old life in sin. You are now conscience and sensitive about your thoughts and behavior of the past. You haven't learned how to deal with those old thoughts and anxieties, but you will learn in time. This new feeling of excitement and tremendous peace and joy has totally consumed you, and it should. This is known as the joy of the Lord, and the peace of God that passes all understanding. This is what is new about you, and it will get better daily. Those old things and ways you have decided to leave behind you. This is what makes you a new creature.

Now remember, the work is not finished: the word has just begun to work within you, and you still must learn how to yield your total mind unto Christ, becoming an instrument in his hand. "We are His workmanship, created in Christ Jesus for good works, which God prepared beforehand that we should walk in them (Ephesians 2:10 N KJV).

> **NOTE:** While you are learning how to walk with Jesus you will come short; not intentionally, it is just learning a new walk. Just get up! Remember the events that brought you to that point and eliminate those fellowships, behaviors, and thoughts. "Let us lay aside every weight, and the sin which doth so easily beset us, and let us run with patience the race that is set before us, looking unto Jesus the author and finisher of our faith; who for the joy that was set before him endured the cross, despising the shame, and is set down at the right hand of the throne of God." (Hebrews 12:1–2 KJV)

The understanding of this new life can clearly be seen as we study the life of the apostle Paul. Therefore, it is mandatory for every new believer to familiarize with Paul's life. The apostle Paul shares his new life transformation and his struggles with the people of God in Romans 7:22–23:

> Objective: (of a person or their judgment) not influenced by personal feelings or opinions in considering and representing biblical facts.

> For I delight in the law of God after the inward man: But I see another law in my members, warring against the law of my mind, and bringing me into captivity to the law of sin which is in my members.

> Romans 7: Please read the whole chapter.

In the Bible, Paul has the most written information concerning this transformation from a life of sin into this life in Christ. As we study these new creatures later in the scripture, they are referred to as ambassadors of Christ. Paul gives an account of his first encounter with the stoning of a believer named Stephen:

> When the blood of thy martyr Stephen was shed, I also was standing by, and

consenting unto his death, and kept the raiment of them that slew him. (Acts 22:20, 7:58 KJV)

Apostle Paul—whose name during the stoning of Stephen was Saul—he knows about a life of sin.

CHAPTER

Signs of Your Newness

*Knowing this, that our old
man is crucified with him, that the
body of sin might be destroyed, that
henceforth we should not serve sin.
—Romans 6:6*

There are several phases to pay attention to while studying this time that will be recur to as the old man and the new man. Paul writes about being a new creature in Christ, referring to phases like "the old man," "the new man," and "the battle within." When the apostle Paul writes the second letter to the church located in Corinth, the Spirit of God moves in him to give clarity to the Conrinthians' new life in Christ. Corinth was a heavily populated metropolitan area, with diverse religious groups, nationalities, and opinions about the news of the death, burial, and resurrection of Jesus.

The first signs of your new creature transformation will begin in your thinking. One of the greatest enemies to your new life will be religious groups' traditions and opinions, of various cultural beliefs. Studying both the Old and New Testament writings is not an option, it is imperative for your understanding. In the New Testament, the books are really letters to the leaders of the people who gathered in that location in each region.

> **WARNING!** Don't be discouraged by the preconceived ideas or opinons of philosophers and people who are ignorant of what the word of God states, from the standpoint of whom the writer is addressing and the reason for the writing. This is what is about to be evident in your life and sometimes these individuals will bring confusing teachings.

Purpose: the reason for which something is done or created or for which something exists.

Jesus spoke in parables to teach spiritual concepts. "My yoke is easy and my burden is light" (Matthew 11:30). Walking with Jesus is easy if you understand the parable and trust his word. The thing that must be understood is how we get yoked up with Jesus so that the burden will not be so challenging. You must understand that there is going to be some resistance—that's what makes it a burden—but if we get in the yoke with Jesus, the burden will become light. How does one get yoked up with Jesus? Studying about yokes is imperative to understand:

> My people are destroyed for lack of knowledge: because thou hast rejected knowledge. (Hosea 4:6 KJV)

When training a new, younger, inexperienced ox how to plow his fields, the farmer yokes the younger ox with the experienced ox. It is the construction of the yoke that is the key to the lesson. The yoke's architectural design is what needs to be studied to understand the lesson. The burden is connected to the yoke, but the weight of the burden rests on the experienced ox's side of the yoke, for him to pull the load. In actuality, the experienced ox could pull the load without any assistance from the younger ox. The lesson of the parable is about the believer walking with Jesus; the moral of the story is that the believer must be yokee together with him to walk with him. If the believer is yoked together with Jesus, the burden is not heavy because Jesus is bearing the weight of the burden. All the believer does is stay in the yoke.

Jesus said to the people concerning the Old Testament:

> Ye have heard that it was said by them of old time, Thou shalt not commit adultery: But I say unto you, That whosoever looketh on a woman to lust after her hath committed adultery with her already in his heart. (Matthew 5:27–28 KJV)

The lesson Jesus is teaching here is a better way to keep the commandments; with the old way, by the time you caught anyone in the act, it was because the sin had already happened in the mind, prior to the manifestation of the act.

The challenge with keeping the law for those in the Old Testament was because they would be thinking about the act, so the violation had been already performed in the mind. This is the process taken before one performs the arousal act in the flesh. Apostle James says it like this:

> Let no man say when he is tempted, I am tempted of God: for God cannot be tempted with evil, neither tempteth he any man: But every man is tempted, when he is drawn away of his own lust, and enticed. Then when lust hath conceived,

it bringeth forth sin: and sin, when it is finished, bringeth forth death. (James 1:13–15 KJV)

So James explains clearly that you are tempted by your own lust and enticed. Keep in mind that it is not sin when it is at the lust stage. At this stage, lust is in the flesh awaiting opportunity from the mind to allow the members of the flesh/body to perform what the flesh/body is lusting for.

> My people destroyed because of the lack of knowledge, resulting in them limiting Christ's working in them and their Kingdom usage.

The *only* way to stop lust from manifesting in the flesh requires a constant studying of yourself, comparing yourself to the word of God.

These things put them in remembrance, charging them before the Lord that they strive not about words to no profit, but to the subverting of the hearers. Study to shew thyself approved unto God, a workman that needeth not to be ashamed, rightly dividing the word of truth. But shun profane and vain babblings. (2 Timothy 2:14–16 KJV)

You *must* study the word of God, measure up to it, and cast down every negative thought that comes into your mind.

> (For the weapons of our warfare are not carnal, but mighty through God to the pulling down of strong holds;) Casting down imaginations, and every high thing that exalteth itself against the knowledge of God, and bringing into captivity every thought to the obedience of Christ" (2 Corinthians 10:4–5 KJV)

Therefore, the believer has to be yoked up with Jesus by the Holy Ghost to walk with him. The Holy Ghost will guide you into all truth.

> I have yet many things to say unto you, but ye cannot bear them now. Howbeit when he, the Spirit of truth, is come, he will guide you into all truth: for he shall not speak of himself; but whatsoever he shall hear, that shall he speak: and he will shew you things to come. He shall glorify me: for he shall receive of mine, and shall shew it unto you. (John 16:12–14 KJV)

In the book of Romans, the seventh chapter, verses 4–25, Paul shares information about the daily challenge of the flesh's warring against the choice to give your life to Jesus. He makes it clear that this is the war that every new believer will be confronted with in his mind:

> When we were in the flesh, the motions of sins, which were by the law, did work in our members to bring forth fruit unto death. But now we are delivered from the law, that being dead wherein we were held; that we should serve in newness of spirit, and not in the oldness of the letter. (Romans 7:4–25 KJV)

Romans 7: Please read the whole chapter.

This chapter, Romans 7:4–25, is one of the best writings of apostle Paul's concerning this battle or war between the flesh and the mind. Paul shares about the emotional roller coaster that every new believer becomes aware of after saying yes to Jesus. Like Paul, you wanted to do what you thought was right to do, but found yourself not doing it. Paul said,

> For to will is present with me; but how to perform that which is good I find not.

> The Greek word for Church is *Ekklesia*, which appears 114 times in 111 New Testament verses.

There will be many scriptures referring to this personal struggle that takes place daily in the mind of every believer; and until the last trumpet sounds we will continue to fight the good fight of faith until we are changed.

CHAPTER

When Will This Battle Cease?

For a moment think about this: The battle in your mind is because the motions of sins stimulate the lust of your flesh. This lust will not cease until you receive your glorious body. Paul writes,

> This I say, brethren, that flesh and blood cannot inherit the kingdom of God; neither doth corruption inherit incorruption. Behold, I shew you a mystery; We shall not all sleep, but we shall all be changed, In a moment, in the twinkling of an eye, at the last trump: for the trumpet shall sound, and the dead shall be raised incorruptible, and we shall be changed. For this corruptible must put on incorruption, and this

mortal must put on immortality. (1 Corinthians 15:50–53 KJV)

This proves that the believer's battle is in the flesh. Consequently, we will have to contend with the flesh, until Jesus returns.

We know that if the earthly tent we live in is destroyed, we have a building from God, an eternal house in heaven, not built by human hands. (2 Corinthians 5:1 KJV)

Definition of Lust: The War against the Mind

> Do not conform to the pattern of this world, but be transformed by the renewing of your mind. Then you will be able to test and approve what God's will is—his good, pleasing and perfect will. (Romans 12:2 NIV)

Lust is defined as a strong craving or desire, often of a sexual nature. The term is used infrequently (twenty-nine times) in scripture. The word is never used in a positive context; rather, it is always seen in a negative light, relating primarily either to a strong desire for sexual immorality or idolatrous worship. In secular literature, the word indicates a strong desire and can carry either good or bad connotations. In these instances, the New International Version does not translate the word as "lust," rather, it is translated as "desire, "longing," and the like. The context surrounding the word lends to this translation in such instances. However, in scripture, as translated in the New International Version, the word is used for a strong desire that is negative and forbidden. Indeed, the unregenerate are governed and controlled by deceitful lusts or desires (Ephesians 2:3, 4:22; Colossians 3:5; Titus 2:12).

Paul uses the word concupiscence in Colossians 3:5; defined as a strong sexual desire, lust, whose synonyms include sexual desire, sexual appetite, sexual longing, ardor, desire, passion, libido, sex drive, sexuality, biological urge, lechery, lasciviousness, and horniness. Therefore, when reading the scriptures, you *must* understand the relationship between the reader of the word and Christ. This information is the reason for the apostle's writing the letter. Therefore, reading, studying, but most of all prayer, are crucial to every believer so that the Spirit of God might open his understanding daily, concerning hidden things about his personal relationships:

> These are the things God has revealed to us by his Spirit. The Spirit searches all things, even the deep things of God. (1 Corinthians 2:10 KJV)

> Our citizenship is in heaven. We eagerly await a Savior from there, the Lord Jesus Christ. (Philippians 3:20)

We will share more concerning this subject of creating new habits in the section **Four Daily New Believer Habits.** Every believer needs to incorporate into the beginning part of his day these habits:

1. Give the Lord your first and best praise of gratitude every morning.
2. Read the scriptures; speak what you read aloud, hearing will reinforce as you read. From your mouth into the atmosphere, to your ear the word of God is your life source and encouragement.
3. Pray, requesting the Lord to open doors of opportunities to be used for his glory. Ask him to help you to be sensitive to the direction of the Holy Spirit.
4. Meditate or reflect silently, sitting still before him for a moment listening, spending a wordless, quiet moment with him before entering the day.

Many of the New Testament writings are credited to the apostle Paul. He authored these letters to the first churches established during the outpouring of the Holy Ghost, as the new blood covenant was being established on the earth among mankind. The newness of grace purchased by the death, burial, and resurrection of Jesus was being offered to all men. These letters were written to those who were experiencing a new relationship with the Lord Jesus Christ; who were, for the most part, already "born again" or had already given their lives to Christ, by the evidence of their receiving the living water Jesus promised.

> He that believeth on me, as the scripture hath said, out of his belly shall flow rivers of living water. (John 7:38–39 KJV)

> . . . the Spirit, which everyone that believe on him should receive.

The apostle Paul states,

> Then they that are in the flesh cannot please God. But ye are not in the flesh, but in the Spirit, if so be that the Spirit of God dwell in you. Now if any man have not the Spirit of Christ, he is none of his. (Romans 8:8–9 KJV)

These writings are not to the world or unbeliever. The Lord had apostle Paul write to the body of Christ the necessary instructions imperative to learn how to walk in this new life with Christ. This new relationship with Christ is called salvation. The transformation of the mind is the act of yielding to Christ. This is the operation every believer is responsible for to be a beneficiary of this plan of salvation. This is where the walk with Jesus first begins; in the inward man.

There will always be a desire within your flesh to fight against your mind. The fight is because of your flesh's disagreement with your mind's choice to walk with Jesus, because the flesh loves the world and the things of the world.

> Everything in the world—the lust of the flesh, the lust of the eyes, and the pride of life—comes not from the Father but from the world. (1 John 2:16 KJV)

Receiving the total Kingdom benefits now.

Walking by the direction given by the Spirit of God, Paul realized that for the new believer to benefit from the salvation purchased by the blood of Jesus, it would be imperative for those who were once without God, to know how to walk with Jesus. There would be resistance from within them (their sinful natures). This battle within each believer is the normal warfare in the flesh of being a new creature in Christ:

> I find this law at work: Although I want to do good, evil is right there with me. (Romans 7:21 21 KJV)

Understand this inward battle; it is because the flesh always wants to return to the previous lustful life of sin. Paul identifies this challenge: "Do not be conformed to this age, but be transformed by the renewing of the mind" (Romans 12:2 INV), if a walk with Jesus will be manifested in the believer's life. This victory to overcome the lust of the flesh is the product won in the battle of the mind; by the casting down of every lustful thought and imagination that is in conflict against your willingness to obey and surrender your body to Jesus.

Apostle Paul dealt with this struggle and concluded that the battle in the flesh is a continuous war within every believer. After encountering this daily battle, the apostle lifted his voice unto the Lord and asked who would deliver him from this body of sin:

> I delight in the law of God after the inward man: But I see another law in my members, warring against the law of my

mind, and bringing me into captivity to the law of sin which is in my members. O wretched man that I am! who shall deliver me from the body of this death? (Romans 7:22–24 KJV)

Paul realized that the resistance was within his own flesh. He wanted every believer to know that within himself is where the rebelliousness is coming from. It is my flesh that wars against my mind's delightful new choice to serve Christ? My flesh is desirous to take my members captive to obey the pleasures of sin again for a season, rather than to allow me to walk with Christ. This battle within us is only because we hunger to walk with Jesus. Therefore, we have to learn how to accomplish this goal to win over the flesh and walk with Jesus. Because I am one of the, "if any man be in Christ, he is a new creature" it will become clearer as we continue.

> You are no longer strangers and foreigners, but fellow citizens of the saints and members of God's household.

I understand now that my transformation of my mind's thinking concerning my old life and old thinking has to change. Even as a new creature my mind is not totally changed, but it has begun. My confession at this moment is, "Lord, my desire is not to do those old things of my past. Lord teach me so that all things will become new. I don't want to do those old lustful things any longer; I want to learn how to walk with you."

CHAPTER

The Necessity of the Promise

This subject concerning the necessity of the promise, and how to receive the Spirit, has become saturated with religious opinions, rather than scriptural support. The subject regarding the promise of the Father is mandatory because the possession of the promise will be privy to divine revelations and clearer understanding. The receiving of this divine gift gives the believer information from the deep mind of God concerning the things God has prepared for those who are heirs and joint-heirs. This information is imperative for the growth of the believer in the establishing of his faith and state of mind in his transformation.

> Let this mind be in you, which was also in Christ Jesus. (Philippians 2:5 KJV)

Walking with Jesus requires a mind transformation. The mind is the center of your overcoming power; it causes the believer to think like Jesus. On numerous times Jesus declared, "I came to do my Father's will." The more familiar you become by reading the word of God, the more you become knowledgeable of the objective and purpose of the will of Jesus and the work he desires to do in your personal life.

Kingdom Thinking is crucial for Kingdom understanding.

Familiarity with the life of Jesus in the scriptures gives the new believer biblical events to meditate on, while giving the Holy Spirit more points of reference to work with in the believer's development of his new mind. This ought to be one of your daily requests: "Lord, I want to do your will." Having this personal mindset and desire will cause your mind transformation to be easier.

> I will give you a new heart and put a new spirit in you; I will remove from you your heart of stone and give you a heart of flesh. (Ezekiel 36:26 KJV)

This will take place more easily if we follow these instructions of apostle Paul:

> Finally, brethren, whatsoever things are true, whatsoever things are honest, whatsoever things are just, whatsoever things are pure, whatsoever things are lovely, whatsoever things are of good report; if there be any virtue, and if there be any praise, think on these things. (Philippians 4:8 KJV)

God is a Spirit, therefore, they who worship him *must* worship him in spirit and in truth (John 4:24). Worshipping God requires faith, transparency, and honesty, and it *must* be done in the Spirit. Worshipping in the Spirit and praying in the Spirit builds your faith (Jude 1:20). Paul reinforces this thought:

> Without faith it is impossible to please him: for he that cometh to God must believe that he is, and that he is a rewarder of them that diligently seek him. (Hebrews 11:6 KJV)

New creatures, a.k.a. ambassadors of Christ. Ambassadors of Christ is the entry level of the personal ministry of everyone who is a new creature in Christ Jesus. This is the day-one mission assignment of every new believer.

As ambassadors, this Holy Spirit information is necessary to understand. For the believer to have true worship, prayer, and a walk with Jesus, having the Holy Spirit is critical. Jesus refers to the Spirit throughout his three-year ministry. Jesus refers to it as the comforter (John 14:26), Spirit of truth (John 16:13), and the living water (John 7:37–39). In the writings to the churches, the apostles refer several times to the work that the Holy Spirit performs in the lives of the children of God.

Jesus Sharing about the Born-Again Experience

In the Gospel according to Saint John, Jesus is recorded directly having an encounter with a man name Nicodemus; this man was one of the leaders of the Pharisees, a religious group of the day. This group, as well as other various religious groups, was constantly challenging the teachings of Jesus. Nicodemus came to Jesus privately by night, wanting to know how to get into the Kingdom of God. Jesus disregard the flattering words of Nicodemus and got directly to the reason he had snuck in by night to meet with him:

> Verily, verily, I say unto thee, except a man be born again, he cannot see the kingdom of God. (John 3:1–3 KJV)

This is the first time that Jesus has used the phrase, "born again." Jesus said first to Nicodemus, "Except a man be born again he cannot see the Kingdom of God."

The second time Jesus says, "Except a man is born again he cannot enter the Kingdom of God." I will revisit this later in this chapter. Jesus continues teaching:

> That which is born of the flesh is flesh; and that which is born of the Spirit is spirit. Marvel not that I said unto thee, Ye must be born again. The wind bloweth where it listeth, and thou hearest the sound thereof, but canst not tell whence it cometh, and whither it goeth: so is every one that is born of the Spirit. Nicodemus answered and said unto him, How can these things be? (John 3:5–9 KJV)

This conversation in the third chapter of St. John continues between Jesus and Nicodemus from verse 2 to verse 21. Jesus stated to him twice his previous statement that "you must be born again." Nicodemus, you must be born again! Marvel not! This was astonishing to the religious leader of the Jews; he personally found it to be phenomenal. Because of the repetition in Jesus' teaching concerning the necessity of being born again, he made being born again synonymous with receiving the Holy Spirit. Here, Jesus takes time to explain as clearly as possible to one of the Jewish religious leaders that the Spirit's operations will be necessary in the life of a born again believer.

Jesus was aware of Nicodemus' difficulty in understanding spiritual teachings with his carnal mind. Apostle Paul writes, ". . . Because the carnal or natural man cannot process spiritual things because they are foolish to him." Jesus asks, "Are you a Master of Israel and know not these things? It is necessary for you to understand the Spiritual operations of being born again." Understanding his confusion, Jesus gave the subject more detail, expanding on the born-again experience that would be imperative for every new believer to enter the Kingdom of God. This was astonishing to the religious leader of the Jews, who found it to be remarkable. Because of the repetition concerning the necessity of receiving the Holy Spirit, the importance of it is obvious. Jesus takes more time to explain as clearly as possible to the religious Jewish leaders. The reason being it would be imperative for every new believer to process the Spirit to enter into Kingdom.

> Kingdom Assignment a task or piece of work assigned to someone as part of a job or course of study.

Before leaving this subject, I want to seize this opportunity to pray that the Spirit might open your understanding concerning the need for the Spirit. Praying in the Spirit will help the believer to become sensitive toward God's voice.

> If we hope for what we do not yet have, we wait for it patiently. In the same way, the Spirit helps us in our weakness. We do not know what we ought to pray for, but the Spirit himself intercedes for us through wordless groans. And he who searches our hearts knows the mind of the Spirit, because the Spirit intercedes for God's people in accordance with the will of God. And we know that in all things God works for the good of those who love him, who have been called according to his purpose. (Romans 8:25–28 KJV)

I will continue to reiterate how much the Spirt of God is mentioned in respect to its association to every believer and his need to receive it. Remember, your transition to becoming a new creature in Christ, having old things passed away and all things being new, requires the operation of the Spirit of Christ within you.

First Repentance, Then Trust in Christ

The "born again" process goes like this! The apostle Paul wrote:

> You should be to the praise of his glory, who first trusted in Christ. In whom ye also trusted, after that ye heard the word of truth, the gospel of your salvation: in whom also after that ye believed, ye were sealed with that holy Spirit of promise, Which is the earnest of our inheritance until the redemption of the purchased possession, unto the praise of his glory. (Ephesians 1:12–14 KJV)

It is the first experience the believer has with God after he trusts in him and gives his life to the Lord.

You first trusted in Christ after you heard the word of truth, the gospel of your salvation (his call to you out of sin); you trusted him. The one who has been called must believe that the invisible God exists. Then the called one must respond to the call of the Lord with the response or answers of repentance. This is the first step towards salvation, recognizing a personal need for forgiveness, when the one who called requests help and forgiveness. (This is called repentance; it is the evidence with open confession and the summation to being water baptized in the Name of Jesus.) God forgives and gives them his Spirit with speaking in tongues (after you believed you were a candidate to be sealed with the holy spirit of promise of your inheritance). Here is another example of some individuals who experienced this trusting of the preached word of the gospel:

> A certain man in Caesarea called Cornelius, a centurion of the band called the Italian band, A devout man, and one that feared God with all his house, which gave much alms to the people, and prayed to God always . . . While Peter yet spake these words, the Holy Ghost fell on all them which heard the word. And they

> of the circumcision which believed were astonished, as many as came with Peter, because that on the Gentiles also was poured out the gift of the Holy Ghost. For they heard them speak with tongues, and magnify God. Then answered Peter, Can any man forbid water, that these should not be baptized, which have received the Holy Ghost as well as we. (Acts 10:1–2 and 44–47 KJV)

Again, Jesus said,

> If ye then, being evil, know how to give good gifts unto your children: how much more shall your heavenly Father give the Holy Spirit to them that ask him. (Luke 11:13 KJV)

In the Gospel of John, he writes,

> Jesus stood and cried, saying, If any man thirst, let him come unto me, and drink. He that believeth on me, as the scripture hath said, out of his belly shall flow rivers of living water. (But this spake he of the Spirit, which they that believe on him should receive: for the Holy Ghost was

not yet given; because that Jesus was not yet glorified.) (John 7:37–39 KJV)

Then, before his ascendance, Jesus gave instruction to his apostles and disciples:

> Repentance and remission of sins should be preached in his name among all nations, beginning at Jerusalem, ye are witnesses of these things. Behold, I send the promise of my Father upon you: but go and wait in the city of Jerusalem, until ye be endued with power from on high. (Luke 24:47–49 KJV)

Let's review some of the apostle Paul's scriptures concerning the Spirit and some of the operations in the life of the believer. Apostle Paul declares that without the Spirit of Christ you do not belong to Christ.

> You are not controlled by your sinful nature. You are controlled by the Spirit if you have the Spirit of God living in you. (And remember that those who do not have the Spirit of Christ living in them do not belong to Christ at all.) (Romans 8:9 KJV)

The Spirit is a gift given to every believer who will ask Jesus for it. The Lord is still giving it to every believer who asks for it.

CHAPTER

Establishing New Believer's Habits

Now that you are a new creature, there must be new habits that will void out those old habits. These new habits will develop and establish your new creature behavior. Many believers are more concerned with the outward appearance, not realizing the Lord is looking at their hearts. Nevertheless, the creationof inward habits will filter into our visible appearances;

> For the LORD seeth not as man seeth; for man looketh on the outward appearance, but the LORD looketh on the heart. (1 Samuel 16:7 KJV)

The *only* way to create new habits is to disassociate yourselves from company that reinforces bad or sinful habits. This includes anything that stimulants thoughts that try to reinforce old behavior in your imagination, television programs, music that takes your mind back to a time and place of fleshly enjoyment, and friends who are not walking with Jesus, but practicing worldly pleasures. Paul mentions a few scriptures concerning this subject:

> Ye were sometimes darkness, but now are ye light in the Lord: walk as children of light: (For the fruit of the Spirit is in all goodness and righteousness and truth;) Proving what is acceptable unto the Lord. And have no fellowship with the unfruitful works of darkness, but rather reprove them. (Ephesians 5:8–11 KJV)

A thought of a friend in your day deserves a contact.

Paul explains that the *only* way to reprove these works of darkness is to cast down these thoughts.

> For the weapons of our warfare are not carnal, but mighty through God to the

pulling down of strong holds; Casting down imaginations, and every high thing that exalteth itself against the knowledge of God, and bringing into captivity every thought to the obedience of Christ. (2 Corinthians 10:4–5 KJV)

The question is, how do you accomplish this? Paul writes,

Brethren, whatsoever things are true, whatsoever things are honest, whatsoever things are just, whatsoever things are pure, whatsoever things are lovely, whatsoever things are of good report; if there be any virtue, and if there be any praise, think on these things. Those things, which ye have both learned, and received, and heard, and seen in me, do: and the God of peace shall be with you. (Philippians 4:8–9 KJV)

It is necessary, therefore, to keep yourself in an environment that is wholesome for your mindset and growth in Christ. Paul writes,

I beseech you therefore, brethren, by the mercies of God, that ye present your bodies

> a living sacrifice, holy, acceptable unto God, which is your reasonable service. And be not conformed to this world: but be ye transformed by the renewing of your mind, that ye may prove what is that good, and acceptable, and perfect, will of God. For I say, through the grace given unto me, to every man that is among you, not to think of himself more highly than he ought to think; but to think soberly, according as God hath dealt to every man the measure of faith. (Romans 12:1–3 KJV)

Then again,

> That ye may approve things that are excellent; that ye may be sincere and without offence till the day of Christ; Being filled with the fruits of righteousness, which are by Jesus Christ, unto the glory and praise of God. (Philippians 1:10–11 KJV)

There are more, but let's end with this one:

> Prove all things; hold fast that which is good. Abstain from all appearance of evil. And the very God of peace sanctify you wholly; and I pray God your whole spirit

and soul and body be preserved blameless unto the coming of our Lord Jesus Christ. (1 Thessalonians 5:21–23 KJV)

Fellowshipping with other believers and attending Bible studies, prayer gatherings, and Sunday services will fortify your desire to build your thinking along with familiarity with the word of God and friendships with members of the body of Christ. Frequent attendance in these settings will strengthen your mind to stand during challenging times away from the body of Christ. Jesus said,

> Kingdom Thinking transforms carnal thinking.

> I pray not that thou shouldest take them out of the world, but that thou shouldest keep them from the evil. They are not of the world, even as I am not of the world. Sanctify them through thy truth: thy word is truth. (John 17:15–17 KJV)

Jesus meant you to represent his glory in the world. Apostle Peter agrees:

> Whereby are given unto us exceeding great and precious promises: that by these

ye might be partakers of the divine nature, having escaped the corruption that is in the world through lust. (2 Peter 1:4 KJV)

Paul urges again with these simple words: "Wherefore come out from among them, and be ye separate, saith the Lord, and touch not the unclean thing; and I will receive you" (2 Corinthians 6:17 KJV), referring to the company the new believer should keep. Then, concerning the importance of obeying the direction of the spirit within: he writes,

As many as are led by the Spirit of God, they are the sons of God. For ye have not received the spirit of bondage again to fear; but ye have received the Spirit of adoption, whereby we cry, Abba, Father. The Spirit itself beareth witness with our spirit, that we are the children of God. (Romans 8:14–16 KJV)

Then apostle John says,

My little children, let us not love in word, neither in tongue; but in deed and in truth. And hereby we know that we are of the truth, and shall assure our hearts before him. For if our heart condemn us, God is greater than our heart, and knoweth all things. Beloved, if our heart condemn us not, then have we confidence toward God. And whatsoever we ask, we receive of him, because we keep his commandments, and do those things that are pleasing in his sight. (1 John 3:18–22 KJV)

Four Daily New Believer Habits

Apostle Paul wanted every believer to understand that there will be a daily battle within you warring against your will to walk with the Lord. In chapter 7 of the book of Romans he clearly lays it out.

> . . . For when we were in the flesh, the motions of sins, which were by the law, did work in our members to bring forth fruit unto death. But now we are delivered from the law, that being dead wherein we were held; that we should serve in newness of spirit, and not in the oldness of the letter. What shall we say

then? Is the law sin? God forbid. Nay, I had not known sin, but by the law: for I had not known lust, except the law had said, Thou shalt not covet. But sin, taking occasion by the commandment, wrought in me all manner of concupiscence. For without the law sin was dead. For I was alive without the law once: but when the commandment came, sin revived, and I died. And the commandment, which was ordained to life, I found to be unto death. For sin, taking occasion by the commandment, deceived me, and by it slew me. Wherefore the law is holy, and the commandment holy, and just, and good. Was then that which is good made death unto me? God forbid. But sin, that it might appear sin, working death in me by that which is good; that sin by the commandment might become exceeding sinful. For we know that the law is spiritual: but I am carnal, sold under sin. For that which I do I allow not: for what I would, that do I not; but what I hate, that do I. If then I do that which I would not, I consent unto the law that it is good. Now then it is no more I that do it, but sin that dwelleth in me. For I know that in me (that is, in my flesh,) dwelleth no good thing: for to will is present with me; but how to perform that which is good I find not. For the good that I would I do not: but the evil which I would not, that I do. Now if I do that I would not, it is no more I that do it, but sin that dwelleth in me. I find then a law, that, when I would do good, evil is present with me. For I delight in the law of God after the inward man: But I see another law in my members, warring against the law of my mind, and bringing me into captivity to the law of sin which is in my members. O wretched man that I am! who shall deliver me from the body of this death? I thank God through Jesus Christ our Lord. So then with the mind I myself serve the law of God; but with the flesh the law of sin. (Romans 7:5–25 KJV)

Romans 7 clearly explains why the believer has to remember that this battle takes place daily. It begins from the time your eyes open each morning until the time you retire at the end of your day, necessarily demanding that new habits be created. These new habits are mandatory to maintain a yielded mind to Jesus. Incorporating these four daily habits is mandatory:

1. Give the Lord your best praise of gratitude. (Psalm 113:3)
2. Read a scripture of your choice; the word of God is your life source.
3. Pray, requesting the Lord to open doors of opportunities to you, to be used by him for his glory. Ask him to help you to be sensitive to the direction of the Holy Spirit. (Jude 1:20)
4. Meditate or reflect silently, sitting still before him for a moment listening. Just spend a wordless, quiet moment with him before entering into the day. (Psalm 1:2)

CHAPTER

God's Ammunition against the Kingdom of Darkness

All things are of God.

Every believer must understand that his previous sinful life experience helps him to share with others his life before Christ and how the Lord changed his life and can do the same for them. It may seem strange, but your old life coupled with your new life can serve as your credentials that qualify you to represent as ambassador of the Kingdom of God. Your new life as a new creature in Christ Jesus qualifies you to share with others. Your old life story allows you to share with others the love of God toward them at this moment. This power to change your life is the ammunition Christ will use for you to share with others, concerning where you were in sin and how the blood of Jesus purchased your new life, forging you of all the wrong done in your past life. Jesus' death on the cross paid in full your forgiveness and freedom from sin, and today you can also be free from the power of sin.

This is powerful. As Paul said,

> I give you to understand, that no man speaking by the Spirit of God calleth Jesus accursed: and that no man can say that Jesus is the Lord, but by the Holy Ghost. (1 Corinthians 12:3 KJV)

Now that you have the saving, life-changing power of the Holy Spirit, you are a witness to the god of this world and his demons. No longer are you under the power of darkness, and you won't stay quiet. Paul encouraged the believer while warning him of this,

> . . . by manifestation of the truth commending ourselves to every man's conscience in the sight of God. But if our gospel be hid, it is hid to them that are lost: In whom the god of this world hath blinded the minds of them which believe not, lest the light of the glorious gospel of Christ, who is the image of God, should

shine unto them. (2 Corinthians 4:2–4 KJV)

You are now the voice of God on the earth to inform the world that this power is available to all who repent and give their lives to Jesus Christ. You have divine revelation and the born-again experiences that qualify you to tell your story to the world. You are Christ's ambassador on the earth. Paul says,

> We are ambassadors for Christ, as though God did beseech you by us: we pray you in Christ's stead, be you reconciled to God. (2 Corinthians 5:20)

There will be much resistance when you share your story of what Jesus has done in your life, by the prince of the power of the air. There will also be those whose minds the god of this world has blinded, so that they are unable to see or understand the gospel of Christ. Many may be friends and loved ones, but you must remember that we do not fight against flesh and blood.

> We wrestle not against flesh and blood, but against principalities, against powers, against the rulers of the darkness of this world. (Ephesians 6:12 KJV)

As ambassadors, when resistance comes we have to listen to the Holy Spirit and let him fight for us. In the Old Testament, Moses tells the people of God, "The LORD your God he shall fight for you" (Exodus 14:14). Then the prophet Ezra declares, "You shall not need to fight in this battle" (2 Chronicles 20:17, 29). The apostle Paul also reminds the new believer how we fight:

> Though we walk in the flesh, we do not war after the flesh: (For the weapons of our warfare are not carnal, but mighty through God to the pulling down of strong holds;) Casting down imaginations, and every high thing that exalteth itself against the knowledge of God, and bringing into captivity every thought to the obedience of Christ. (2 Corinthian 10:3–5 KJV)

. . . a made up mind to serve Kingdom Thinking

The apostle Paul is the apostle to the Gentiles, which is very interesting because he was a master of the law of Moses, yet he was not a believer in Jesus originally. it was after his transformation from religious Judaism and his becoming a believer in Christ Jesus that he began to share the gospel. Afterward, when Jesus commissioned him, he began to write to the saints of Jesus in his many letters, announcing,

> I might also have confidence in the flesh. If any other man thinketh that he hath whereof he might trust in the flesh, I more: Circumcised the eighth day, of the stock of Israel, of the tribe of Benjamin, a Hebrew of the Hebrews; as touching the law, a Pharisee; Concerning zeal, persecuting the church; touching the righteousness which is in the law, blameless. But what things were gain to me, those I counted loss for Christ. (Philippians 3:4–7 KJV)

Jesus called him and sent him to the nations that were referred to as heathens or dogs by Jesus (Matthew 15:26). All the nations that were not Hebrews were known in those days to be Gentiles. The previous life of Paul, before Jesus called him, runs parallel with all of our lives. It was the state of mind of all those whom Jesus brought out of their sinful lives of darkness, and who now stand in his marvelous light. Therefore, I am using the apostle Paul as our prime example in this book. The days or events in your life prior to your surrendering your life to Jesus are crucial to remember. This is the time before you became a new creature. You had to repent, from your sins and the life you lived, while being willing to repent and follow Jesus. Paul puts it like this:

> We should be to the praise of his glory, who first trusted in Christ. (Ephesians 1:12–13 KJV)

God Has Hidden Things Just to Be Revealed to You

Paul explains that we were those who were without God, godless:

> We are his workmanship, created in Christ Jesus unto good works, which God hath before ordained that we should walk in them. Wherefore remember, that ye being in time past Gentiles in the flesh, who are called Uncircumcision by that which is called the Circumcision in the flesh made by hands; That at that time ye were without Christ, being aliens from the commonwealth of Israel, and strangers from the covenants of promise, having no hope, and without God in the world:

But now in Christ Jesus ye who sometimes were far off are made nigh by the blood of Christ. (Ephesians 2:10–13 KJV)

Understand, giving your life to Jesus was a serious choice made with a broken heart and reaching hands requesting his help. It was in this moment that real transformation began, and it is not finished. You want the Lord to give you the promise of the Holy Spirit; do not settle for anything less than receiving it like those in the upper room (Acts 2:4), or those at Cornelius' house (Acts 10:1,44–46), or when apostle Paul found certain disciples at Corinth (Acts 19:1–6).

That is why he continues in Ephesians to share with the new believer concerning the seal of validation of our trusting Christ:

In whom ye also trusted, after that ye heard the word of truth, the gospel of your salvation: in whom also after that ye believed, ye were sealed with that holy Spirit of promise, Which is the earnest of our inheritance until the redemption of the purchased possession, unto the praise of his glory. (Ephesians 1:14 KJV)

The Holy Spirit of promise is the earnest of our inheritance that the believers were sealed with, a seal that is good until the redemption of the purchased possession. (Ephesians 1:12–14 KJV)

Paul declares that many scholars, false teachers, Pharisees, Sadducees, and even the religious orders of today would attempt to look into the hidden treasures of God, but he has hidden them from them, to reveal them to his people.

Listen as you read:

But as it is written, Eye hath not seen, nor ear heard, neither have entered into the heart of man, the things which God hath prepared for them that love him. But God hath revealed them unto us by his Spirit: for the Spirit searcheth all things, yea, the deep things of God. For what man knoweth the things of a man, save the spirit of man which is in him? even so the things of God knoweth no man, but the Spirit of God. Now we have received, not the spirit of the world, but the spirit which is of God; that we might know the things that are freely given to us of God, (1 Corinthians 2:9–12 KJV)

So the spirit of promise is so God can let you in on the deep things that he has hidden from the world reserved to be revealed just to those who have his Spirit. Just for you! Isn't that awesome?

> Receiving the total Kingdom benefits from God, as a man thinks.

A Little More about the Apostle to the Gentiles

This information is extremely important to everyone who is not a Hebrew of the lineage of Abraham, Isaac, and Jacob. If you find yourself in this category, which Paul spoke about in the book of Ephesians, and now have given your life to Jesus, you are one of the new creatures in Christ. Look at your state before you became a beneficiary of the death, burial, and resurrection of Jesus. But now:

> We are his workmanship, created in Christ Jesus unto good works" (you may be in the beginning stages but, nevertheless, new) "which God hath before ordained that we should walk in them. Wherefore remember, that ye being in time past Gentiles in the flesh, who are called Uncircumcision

> by that which is called the Circumcision in the flesh made by hands; That at that time ye were without Christ, being aliens from the commonwealth of Israel, and strangers from the covenants of promise, having no hope, and without God in the world: But now in Christ Jesus ye who sometimes were far off are made nigh by the blood of Christ. (Ephesians 2:12 KJV)

The Apostle Paul was a very interesting apostle. He said of himself that he was born out of due time. In actuality, he was informing us that concerning following and obeying Jesus, he was also a beneficiary of the salvation found in the blood of Jesus. He wants the readers to know and understand that he also was a sinful creature. And now, just like Paul, you who were once lost in sin are now new creatures. There will now be things you will eventually learn about yourself and Jesus by the Spirit within you. There will be times when being new will seem to be extremely unlikely, because your old man behavior and desires will seem to bombard your mind. Nevertheless, you are what Christ said you are; you just need to look closer.

How do you feel about sin now? Remember, you used to live in it without giving your behavior any consideration. But now you are troubled within your mind concerning your thought behaviors. That's new! (Remember Romans chapter 7.) Not only is that new, it is also the first sign that you are new yet not finished.

> It is God which worketh in you both to will and to do of his good pleasure. (Phil 2:13 KJV)

You must understand this: The "I want to do right" thing going over and over in your mind is really not you, it is Jesus working in you. When you mess up, ask the Lord to forgive you right away; he has promised to do that.

This walk with Jesus is a battle in your mind. The apostles Paul and John help us to understand this. Paul writes, in the book of Romans,

> If then I do that which I would not, I consent unto the law that it is good. Now then it is no more I that do it, but sin that dwelleth in me. For I know that in me (that is, in my flesh,) dwelleth no good thing: for to will is present with me; but how to perform that which is good I find not. (Romans 7:16–18 KJV)

This chapter helps us understand the daily challenge that everyone has in the flesh, from the time we rise in the morning to the time we retire for the evening. We don't entertain the thought, we cast the thought down.

> Casting down imaginations, and every high thing that exalteth itself against the knowledge of God, and bringing into captivity every thought to the obedience of Christ. (2 Corinthians 10:5 KJV)

Then we follow the instructions of the Apostle John:

> If we say that we have no sin, we deceive ourselves, and the truth is not in us. If we confess our sins, he is faithful and just to forgive us our sins, and to cleanse us from all unrighteousness. (1 John 1:8–9 KJV)

When we encounter one of these battles, Paul declares in the letter to Corinth, concerning himself,

> He was seen of above five hundred brethren at once; of whom the greater part remains unto this present, but some are

fallen asleep. After that, he was seen of James; then of all the apostles. And last of all he was seen of me also, as of one born out of due time. For I am the least of the apostles, that am not meet to be called an apostle, because I persecuted the church of God. But by the grace of God I am what I am: and his grace which was bestowed upon me was not in vain; but I laboured more abundantly than they all: yet not I, but the grace of God which was with me. Therefore, whether it were I or they, so we preach, and so ye believed. (1 Corinthians 15:6–11 KJV)

This brings us to the subject concerning who you are in Christ. In Corinthians, apostle Paul expands on the new life in Christ with additional information. He states that believers are the workmanship of Christ. They are no longer alienated from all of the commonwealth and covenant promises God gave to Abraham. They are no longer without God in the world. Now, because of the blood of Jesus they are made nigh to Christ. Now, the apostle Paul wants new believers to understand, that they are recipients of salvation purchased by the blood of Jesus.

> If any man be in Christ, he is a new creature: old things are passed away; behold, all things are become new. And all things are of God, who hath reconciled us to himself by Jesus Christ, and hath given to us the ministry of reconciliation; To wit, that God was in Christ, reconciling the world unto himself, not imputing their trespasses unto them; and hath committed unto us the word of reconciliation. Now then we are ambassadors for Christ, as though God did beseech you by us: we pray you in Christ's stead, be ye reconciled to God. For he hath made him to be sin for us, who knew no sin; that we might be made the righteousness of God in him. (2 Corinthians 5:17–21 KJV)

> **You are no longer strangers and foreigners, but fellow citizens of the saints and members of God's household.**

Therefore, it must be understood that your previous sinful life is forgiven. This experience qualifies you to share the gospel of new life as a new creature in Christ Jesus. This is the story you will use against demonic forces as you share with others concerning the redemption, reconciling the purchased power of the blood of Jesus that he paid on the cross to free the believers from the power of sin. This is powerful, Paul said,

> I give you to understand, that no man speaking by the Spirit of God calleth Jesus accursed: and that no man can say that Jesus is the Lord, but by the Holy Ghost. (1 Corinthians 12:3 KJV)

Now, because you have the saving, life-changing power of the Holy Spirit, you can share that this power is available to all; those who are in relationship with Jesus Christ. You have divine revelation concerning who Jesus is that qualifies you to represent the Kingdom of Christ as an ambassador, to tell your story!

CHAPTER

Your Damascus Road

Who hath reconciled us to
himself by Jesus Christ . . .

Your previous life style and your present commitment to Christ will cause friends who know you to inquire concerning your choice to follow Jesus. Apostle Paul experienced the same from those who knew him from the time he appeared on the scene at the stoning of a man named Stephen (Acts 22:20). Paul was a young man, then named Saul, watching as the religious leaders of the day confronted Stephen for following Jesus. Stephen was a beneficiary of the grace of God. After witnessing this unrighteous death, Saul became an activist for the cause of Judaism against the grace move of Jesus:

> I persecuted this way unto the death, binding and delivering into prisons both men and women. As also the high priest doth bear me witness, and all the estate of the elders: from whom also I received letters unto the brethren, and went to Damascus, to bring them which were there bound unto Jerusalem, for to be punished. (Acts 22:4 KJV)

Then, on his way to Damascus, he had an encounter with Jesus:

> It came to pass, that, as I made my journey, and was come nigh unto Damascus about noon, suddenly there shone from heaven a great light round about me. And I fell unto the ground, and heard a voice saying unto me, Saul, Saul, why persecutest thou me? And I answered, Who art thou, Lord? And he said unto me, I am Jesus of Nazareth, whom thou persecutest. And they that were with me saw indeed the light, and were afraid; but they heard not the voice of him that spake to me. And I said, What shall I do, Lord? And the Lord said unto me, Arise, and go into Damascus; and there it shall be told

thee of all things which are appointed for thee to do. And when I could not see for the glory of that light, being led by the hand of them that were with me, I came into Damascus. And one Ananias, a devout man according to the law, having a good report of all the Jews which dwelt there, Came unto me, and stood, and said unto me, Brother Saul, receive thy sight. And the same hour I looked up upon him. (Acts 22:6–13 KJV)

After this event, Paul became a beneficiary, teacher, and the apostle to the Gentiles, telling how the grace of God was bestowed upon him as an unrighteous man. His eyes were opened concerning his prior accusation between the laws of Moses and Jesus, and he clearly demonstrated the accusation in his teachings and letters to the churches. God's grace, mercy, and love toward him are recorded in his letters to the churches, as well as his personal testimonies given before municipalities. Paul confessed that he was zealous in his faithfulness to the religious traditions of his fathers, faithful to the religious beliefs taught to him by the fathers who practiced Judaism. Their teachings taught that the followers of Jesus were blasphemers for their support and worship of him.

Therefore, Paul persecuted the believers and followers of Jesus, reminding all those who had heard of him,

> Ye have heard of my conversation in time past in the Jews' religion, how that beyond measure I persecuted the church of God, and wasted it: And profited in the Jews' religion above many my equals in mine own nation, being more exceedingly zealous of the traditions of my fathers. (Galatians 1:13–14 KJV)

> Kingdom thinking is superior to religious thinking.

The Resistance of Your Faith in God's Word

Paul declares,

> Do I now persuade men, or God? or do I seek to please men? for if I yet pleased men, I should not be the servant of Christ. But I certify you, brethren, that the gospel which was preached of me is not after man. For I neither received it of man, neither was I taught it, but by

the revelation of Jesus Christ. But when it pleased God, who separated me from my mother's womb, and called me by his grace, To reveal his Son in me, that I might preach him among the heathen; immediately I conferred not with flesh and blood. (Galatians1:10–16 KJV)

Then, in another place, he writes,

I am the least of the apostles, who am not fit to be called apostle, because I have persecuted the assembly of God. But by God's grace I am what I am; and his grace, which [was] towards me, has not been vain; but I have laboured more abundantly than they all, but not I, but the grace of God which [was] with me. (1 Corinthians 15:9–10 Darby)

Apostle Paul testify throughout his writings:

He states his Jewish inheritance born in Tarsus, a city in Cilicia. Schooled by Gamaliel one of the greatest scholars of his day, and taught according to the perfect manner of the law of the fathers. He was zealous toward God, and his persecuted the church of Christ. Responsible for the death of many, while also binding and delivering many to prisons both men and women. Letting them know that he was supported by the high priest and the elders. Receiving letters to bring the believers which were abroad to be brought to Jerusalem to be punished. As I made one of my journey to Damascus about noon, suddenly there shone from heaven a great light round about me, I fell onto the ground. A voice said unto me, Saul, Saul, why persecutes thou me? I answered, Who art thou, Lord? He said unto me, I am Jesus of Nazareth, who you are persecuting. And the Lord said unto me, Arise, and go into Damascus; and there it shall be told thee of all things which are appointed for thee to do. (Acts 22:3–10)

CHAPTER

The Ministry of Reconciliation

. . . and hath given to us the ministry of reconciliation.

A preconceived idea of what ministry really is will cause many to miss what the objective of ministry is in their personal lives for Christ. We pray that the Spirit of Christ opens your eyes concerning the hidden divine plan of God for you and others in these last days! You are anointed to tell your story about your transformation from your life of sin into your present relationship in Christ. This is not a new plan, because there's nothing new under the sun. King Solomon in the book of Ecclesiastes says,

> History merely repeats itself. It has all been done before. Nothing under the sun is truly new. (Ecclesiastes 1:9 NLT)

> Your personal story never becomes out dated or old

What we are about to share is that the body of Christ conception, after his death, burial, and resurrection, is about to receive a reboot by the spirit of God in the last days on the earth. Remember, God told us that before that he would do a thing that he would tell us! The prophet Isaiah declares it:

> Behold, the former things are come to pass, and new things do I declare: before they spring forth I tell you of them. (Isaiah 42:9 KJV)

One of the new things is the releasing of divine hidden knowledge to the people of God concerning a forgotten move of God in the past.

The Created Situation That Caused a Move of God (Part 1)

When we look at the birth of the church on the day of Pentecost, we think of the upper room where Jesus told the disciples to go and wait until they received the promise of the Father (Luke 24:49). After being there for ten days, a sound came from heaven; this is the event that Jesus shared with

Nicodemus (John 3:8, Acts 2:2). There was a multitude of nations and people there because it was the Jewish celebration of the time of Pentecost. This is amazing when you understand what this Jewish feast meant to Israel.

Why on the Day of Pentecost?

If you go back and read the Old Testament, you will discover that Pentecost was one of the Jewish feast days. Only they didn't call it Pentecost; that's the Greek name. The Jews called it the Feast of Harvest or the Feast of Weeks. It is mentioned five places in the first five books—in Exodus 23, Exodus 24, Leviticus 16, Numbers 28, and Deuteronomy 16. It was the celebration of the beginning of the early weeks of harvest. In Palestine there were two harvests each year. The early harvest came during the months of May and June; the final harvest came in the fall. Pentecost was the celebration of the beginning of the early wheat harvest, which meant that Pentecost fell sometime during the middle of the month of May or early June.

There were several festivals, celebrations, or observances that took place before Pentecost. There was Passover, there was the Feast of Unleavened Bread, and there was the Feast of First Fruits.

The Feast of First Fruits was the celebration of the beginning of the barley harvest. Here's the way you figured out the date of Pentecost: According to the Old Testament, you would go to the day of the celebration of First Fruits and, beginning with that day, you would count off fifty days. The fiftieth day would be the Day of Pentecost. So First Fruits is the beginning of the barley harvest, and Pentecost the celebration of the beginning of the wheat harvest. Since it was always fifty days after First Fruits, and since fifty days equals seven weeks, it always came a "week of weeks" later. Therefore, they either called it the Feast of Harvest or the Feast of Weeks. There are three things you need to know about Pentecost that will help you understand Acts 2.

> Pentecost is not a religion it is a experience

Pentecost was a pilgrim festival. That meant that according to Jewish Law, all the adult Jewish men would come from wherever they were living to Jerusalem and personally be in attendance every year during this celebration. During this holiday, no servile work was to be done, school was out, and the shops were closed. It was party time. There were certain celebrations and sacrifices and offerings which were prescribed in the Law for the day of Pentecost. In the Old Testament, the high priest was to take two loaves of freshly baked wheat bread and offer them before the Lord. The wheat bread was made from the newly harvested wheat. In short, Pentecost in the time of the Apostles was a great and grand harvest celebration. The streets of Jerusalem were clogged with thousands of pilgrims who had come from every point of the compass to celebrate the goodness of God and the bringing in of the wheat harvest.

Why This Day of Pentecost has Great Significance?

There was also the Jubilee year. This is the year at the end of seven cycles of Sabbatical years and, according to Biblical regulations, it had a special impact on the ownership and management of land in the Land of Israel. Jubilee deals largely with land, property, and property rights. According to Leviticus, slaves and prisoners would be freed, debts would be forgiven, and the mercies of God would be particularly manifest. Leviticus 25:8–13 states:

> You shall count off seven Sabbaths of years, seven times seven years; and there shall be to you the days of seven Sabbaths of years, even forty-nine years. Then you

shall sound the loud trumpet on the tenth day of the seventh month. On the Day of Atonement you shall sound the trumpet throughout all your land. You shall make the fiftieth year holy, and proclaim liberty throughout the land to all its inhabitants. It shall be a jubilee to you; and each of you shall return to his own property, and each of you shall return to his family. That fiftieth year shall be a jubilee to you. In it you shall not sow, neither reap that which grows of itself, nor gather from the undressed vines. For it is a jubilee; it shall be holy to you. You shall eat of its increase out of the field. In this Year of Jubilee each of you shall return to his property.

Here Pentecost is referring to the spiritual realm, the manifested promise that God made in the garden:

I will put enmity between you and the woman, and between your offspring and hers; he will crush your head, and you will strike his heel. (Genesis 3:15)

This is the deal God promised. The blood of Jesus purchased back ownership of man from sin and the devil. The promise of the Father will now manage the land and earthen vessels of man and man's property rights. The Lord will by the promise of the Father set the slaves and prisoners of sin free. Because the blood of Jesus paid the debts for the wages of sin, they who receive him have been forgiven. By receiving the promise of the Father, you are beneficiary of God's mercies.

Jesus purchased mankind's restoration by the blood shed on the cross, to restore their original relationship with God upon the earth. Now the believer has power to walk in the original plan of authority and power God designed man to initially walk in!

Let's continue to review the move of God on the day of Pentecost when the Holy Ghost or promise of the Father filled the upper room where the disciples were sitting. The major event was noised abroad:

> There were dwelling at Jerusalem Jews, devout men, out of every nation under heaven. Now when this was noised abroad, the multitude came together, and were confounded, because that every man

heard them speak in his own language. And they were all amazed and marvelled, saying one to another, Behold, are not all these which speak Galilaeans? And how hear we every man in our own tongue, wherein we were born? Parthians, and Medes, and Elamites, and the dwellers in Mesopotamia, and in Judaea, and Cappadocia, in Pontus, and Asia, Phrygia, and Pamphylia, in Egypt, and in the parts of Libya about Cyrene, and strangers of Rome, Jews and proselytes, Cretes and Arabians, we do hear them speak in our tongues the wonderful works of God. And they were all amazed, and were in doubt, saying one to another, What meaneth this? Others mocking said, These men are full of new wine. But Peter, standing up with the eleven, lifted up his voice, and said unto them, Ye men of Judaea, and all ye that dwell at Jerusalem, be this known unto you, and hearken to my words: For these are not drunken, as ye suppose, seeing it is but the third hour of the day. But this is that which was spoken by the prophet Joel; And it shall come to pass in the last days, saith God, I will pour out of my Spirit upon all flesh: and your sons and your daughters shall prophesy, and your young men shall see visions, and your old men shall dream dreams: And on my servants and on my handmaidens I will pour out in those days of my Spirit; and they shall prophesy. (Acts 2:5–18 KJV)

> About fifteen dialects from various regions made up the languages spoken in the upper room.

Reading the book of Acts will explain the event of persecution that came upon the church during its beginning. Everyone who received the promise of the Father in the upper room remained in Jerusalem, and Jesus said,

> Being assembled together with them, commanded them that they should not depart from Jerusalem, but wait for the promise of the Father, which, saith he, ye have heard of me. For John truly baptized with water; but ye shall be baptized with the Holy Ghost not many days hence. When they therefore were come together, they asked of him, saying, Lord, wilt thou at this time restore again the kingdom to Israel? And he said unto them, It is not for you to know the times or the seasons,

which the Father hath put in his own power. But ye shall receive power, after that the Holy Ghost is come upon you: and ye shall be witnesses unto me both in Jerusalem, and in all Judaea, and in Samaria, and unto the uttermost part of the earth. (Acts 1:4–8 KJV)

So along comes Saul to persecute the church causing them to flee for their lives, all except the apostles. Saul was God's instrument to move his people from their comfort zone in Jerusalem, remember, "ye shall be witnesses unto me both in Jerusalem, and in all Judaea, and in Samaria, and unto the uttermost part of the earth." Not until the persecution of Saul came upon the church were they scattered abroad. The thing to remember is; not all of them, all of the apostles stayed. You must note that the apostles stayed in Jerusalem, even when Saul became the enemy of the church; the church didn't understand that Saul was God's man. Yes, as a witness at the stoning of Stephen with a front-row seat where the participants in the stoning laid their coats at his feet. His name was Saul (a name meaning

> You can be used by God from wherever you were called from.

Destroyer). Saul was in the hand of God to drive the church in Jerusalem abroad. Then God would call him later, to be converted to Christianity after his experience on the road to Damascus (Acts 9).

CHAPTER

Your Real Story

*. . . and hath committed unto
us the word of reconciliation.*

Your ability to articulate your born-again or new-found relationship in Christ is called the word of reconciliation. It is your story told that causes hearers to want to give their lives to Jesus also. This doesn't require a vast knowledge of the scriptures. Nor does it require ministerial classes or credentials to tell your story. When Jesus called Paul to become the apostle to the Gentiles later in his conversion (Romans 11:13), he changed his name from Saul to Paul (a name meaning Builder). God takes the destroyer (Saul) of Acts 8:1 and makes him the apostle to the Gentiles, who wrote two-thirds of the New Testament. This transition of apostle Paul into the Kingdom of Christ or Christianity made him an instrument in the hand

from a Godless minded person to a Kingdom Thinking Ambassador for Christ

of Christ; working together with God to win the world.

This is why God wants to use you also. Like Paul, you have a real story of redemption to tell. You have been reconciled by the blood of Jesus, and sealed by the Spirit of God. This is why your story when told is called the ministry of reconciliation. You may feel that you are not qualified, but no one can tell your story like you but you. Paul explains the Kingdom operation's administrated system of God to win the world. Apostle Paul writes,

> Christ gave some, apostles; and some, prophets; and some, evangelists; and some, pastors and teachers. Then he explains why? . . . For the perfecting of the saints, for the work of the ministry, for the edifying of the body of Christ. (Ephesians 4:11–12)

CHAPTER

The Witness

To wit, that God was in Christ, reconciling the world unto himself . . . The Mystery of the Love of God

You may not understand how it happened, but you know something happened. You know that you have been reconciled if you are searching the relevance of your personal place in the Kingdom of God or are desirous of a detailed explanation "why God gave his son to save me." This question may prove to be an eye-opening, mind-blowing, personal revelation experience. The asking of this question is the first step to divine revelation knowledge concerning who Christ is. Rule of thumb: "For the Spirit of God to reveal a divine purpose to you, you must first be able to frame the question." This question may very well be the platform on which the total agenda for the divine plan of God rests. To understand the answer will open the eyes of many believers to see their Kingdom value, what they offer to the Kingdom and his salvation plan. The answer also will explain the benefits purchased, by the death, burial, and resurrection of Jesus. It will also reveal the purpose of the believer's call and the objective of his calling in relationship with Jesus. This personal information will give clarity to every believer concerning his salvation assignment in the big picture of the Kingdom of God.

Think how patient God was to bring you to this state of mind.

The value to a thing is determined by its rarity and cost. The value of our salvation is also determined by its rarity and its cost. There is a saying in Christianity that salvation is free! This statement is extremely misleading, it cost Jesus his life to purchase salvation's restoring man's relationship with God again. This is the ultimate price? To benefit from the purchasing of the plan of salvation will also cost the benefiters to participate in the price of the salvation plan. Everyone who wants to be a partaker in the plan of salvation *must* surrender himself to the purchaser. Therefore, the plan of salvation is a tradeoff: "Jesus gave his life for us; now we are to give our life to him." This is the value every believer personally brings to Jesus in exchange to receive salvation or Kingdom's benefits.

Your greatest asset you bring to Jesus is your willingness to allow him to work in you. He has already paid the price for the sins of the world in full. Give him your broken, sinful life and willingness to surrender to the will of God. Apostle Paul shares this dilemma from our old life into this new relationship with Christ:

> You should know that the unrighteous shall not inherit the kingdom of God? Be not deceived: neither fornicators, nor idolaters, nor adulterers, nor effeminate, nor abusers of themselves with mankind, nor thieves, nor covetous, nor drunkards, nor revilers, nor extortioners, shall inherit the kingdom of God. (1 Corinthians 6:9–10)

Then Paul reminds us of our condition before yielding our body/members unto Christ:

> Such were some of us: but now we are washed, are sanctified, and are justified in the name of the Lord Jesus, and by the Holy Spirit of our God. (1 Corinthians 6:11)

Now, the work of Christ within us by the Holy Spirit starts working on our sinful thinking by establishing new thoughts of life as the believer casts down thoughts of death, with this understanding of the authority and power that the believer possesses in Christ. Paul then reminds us of the fight within every believer for the mind. He says, "All things are lawful unto me, but all things are not expedient: all things are lawful for me, but I will not be brought under the power of any, because I am free in Christ dead to sin and alive in Christ. (1Corinthians 6:12 KJV)

The part you contribute to salvation is your willingness to allow Christ to finish the work he began in you (Philippians 1:6). Jesus will work his renewal plan of salvation in your life if you yield to him your members. This yielding, reading, and prayer is how we assist Christ in the transformation of our mind. "Do not be conformed to this age, but be transformed by the renewing of your mind, so that you may discern what is the good, pleasing, and perfect will of God." By yielding our minds to Christ in reading and prayer, we allow Christ to work in us by the Holy Spirit. This is how Christ works the transformation in our thinking from darkness (dark thinking) into the light thinking of his Kingdom.

This is how we walk with Jesus. It's a two-step program in the beginning.

Step one: 2 Corinthians 10:5
Step two: Philippians 4:8

All Jesus wants the believers to do is willingly surrender their messed-up thinking of sin to him. Jesus wants to forgive them and clean them up by his blood (Spirit) to give salvation and peace that will glorify his name making them his glorious workmanship. We are to give ourselves to Jesus, and he is going to work transformations in our lives. This is how we are "working with God to win the world," understanding that God is trying to win souls by the changing of our lives for his glory. For Jesus to say that he has power to save men and bring them out of sin into his marvelous light, he needs willing individuals so that he can showcase their new lives in the world. Walking with Jesus is not a one-event or one-step program. It is the willing surrender of our minds to Jesus. Those who really love the Lord can do this! The conclusion of the matter is that you have the authority and power to say no! Just as you said no to the devil and repented, you still have the power to say no to sin; and yes to Jesus, allowing him to have his way in your life. Understanding that your members are now his; you are his temple.

CHAPTER

Remembering You Were Forgiven

... not imputing their
trespasses unto them.

And she shall bring forth a son, and thou shalt call his name JESUS: for he shall save his people from their sins. Now all this was done, that it might be fulfilled which was spoken of the Lord by the prophet, saying, Behold, a virgin shall be with child, and shall bring forth a son, and they shall call his name Emmanuel, which being interpreted is, God with us. (Matthew 1:21–23 KJV)

This is the key to God's forgiving us of our trespasses. This was the amazing fascination that caused apostle Paul to be so faithful to the Lord Jesus Christ.

> Blessed are those whom God remembers their sins no more.

Paul understood the Old Testament writing of King David and the prophet Isaiah: "Blessed is he whose transgression is forgiven, whose sin is covered. Blessed is the man unto whom the LORD imputeth not iniquity, and in whose spirit there is no guile" (Ps 32:1–2 KJV) and, "I, even I, am he that blotteth out thy transgressions for mine own sake, and will not remember thy sins" (Isaiah 43:25 KJV). Apostle Paul began to understand the sayings of the prophets of old, whom he had study as a youth:

> I have blotted out, as a thick cloud, thy transgressions, and, as a cloud, thy sins: return unto me; for I have redeemed thee. Sing, O ye heavens; for the LORD hath done it: shout, ye lower parts of the earth: break forth into singing, ye mountains, O forest, and every tree therein: for the LORD hath redeemed Jacob, and glorified himself in Israel. Thus saith the LORD, thy redeemer, and he that formed thee from the womb, I am the LORD that maketh all things; that stretcheth forth the heavens alone; that spreadeth abroad the earth by myself. (Isaiah 44:22–24 KJV)

In the letter to the church in Rome, Paul writes,

> As David also describeth the blessedness of the man, unto whom God imputeth righteousness without works, Saying, Blessed are they whose iniquities are forgiven, and whose sins are covered. Blessed is the man to whom the Lord will not impute sin. (Romans 4:6–8 KJV)

CHAPTER

Your Kingdom Ambassador Credentials

We are ambassadors for
Christ, as though God did
beseech you by us.

The apostle John agrees with the apostle Paul concerning the state of the believer's office on the earth. John declares,

> They are not of the world, even as I am not of the world. Sanctify them through thy truth: thy word is truth. As thou hast sent me into the world, even so have I also sent them into the world. (John 17:16–18 KJV)

The believers are no longer of the world even though they are in the world. They are now heirs and join heirs in the Kingdom of God. As Jesus represented his father on the earth we now, also represent Jesus on the earth. We are Kingdom citizens. Our Kingdom citizenship position allows us to be recognized under the laws as being citizens of the Kingdom of Christ. This qualifies the believer to represent Christ on the earth as an ambassador, because we now have our citizenship in another country, the Kingdom of God. And as ambassadors we are accredited diplomats sent by the head of the Kingdom of Heaven to be Jesus' official representative on the earth (in this example, another country).

The Kingdom citizenship challenges are made clear by the Apostle John. We are not of the world, even as the Lord is not of the world. Therefore, we are hated in the world. We have been given the word of God; and the word of God is manifested in us. The world hated Jesus, because he is the light of the world; the world will hate you because he, Jesus, is in you. But you must understand it is not you that they hate; it is the manifested word of God in your life, which is Jesus, that the world hates. So the conclusion is that our being in the world but not

> My kingdom is not of this world: if my kingdom were of this world, then would my servants fight, that I should not be delivered to the Jews. St John 18:36

of the world is our assignment in the world until Jesus arrives to represent the Kingdom of God on the earth. We do this by letting our light shine in the world and walking in the office of ambassadors.

Both Paul and Peter established this concept concerning the children of God's new citizenship and positions; as ambassadors and as members of a chosen generation and a holy nation in the Kingdom of Christ.

> [God] hath given to us the ministry of reconciliation; To wit, that God was in Christ, reconciling the world unto himself, not imputing their trespasses unto them; and hath committed unto us the word of reconciliation. Now then we are ambassadors for Christ, as though God did beseech you by us. (2 Corinthians 5:18–20 KJV)

Paul explains to the church in Philippians,

> Our conversation [citizenship] is in heaven; from whence also we look for the Savior, the Lord Jesus Christ: Who shall change our vile body, that it may be fashioned like unto his glorious body, according to the working whereby he

> An ambassador can't officially represent in the country of their citizenship.

is able even to subdue all things unto himself. (Philippians 3:20–21 KJV)

Apostle Peter also gives clarity to who we are as children of God in the Kingdom and Christ's objective that he desires to perform in us on the earth:

> Ye are a chosen generation, a royal priesthood, an holy nation, a peculiar people; that ye should shew forth the praises of him who hath called you out of darkness into his marvelous light. (1 Peter 2:9)

Ambassadors' Kingdom Benefits

The word of God is the model for any governmental Kingdom structure. In the Kingdom, the King supplies the needs for both the citizens and the ambassadors. This is the faith operating Kingdom:

> When thou prayest, thou shalt not be as the hypocrites are: for they love to pray standing in the synagogues and in the corners of the streets, that they may be

seen of men. Verily I say unto you, They have their reward. But thou, when thou prayest, enter into thy closet, and when thou hast shut thy door, pray to thy Father which is in secret; and thy Father which seeth in secret shall reward thee openly. But when ye pray, use not vain repetitions, as the heathen do: for they think that they shall be heard for their much speaking. Be not ye therefore like unto them: for your Father knoweth what things ye have need of, before ye ask him. (Matthew 6:5–8 KJV)

The confidence of all of the citizens in the Kingdom must have the same mindset that our King will provide all our needs. In the case of the ambassadors representing the king and his Kingdom, the King provides all for their services: housing, medical, food, clothing, transportation, and diplomatic immunity, to name a few things. This is the promise that Jesus made to all who choose to follow him:

> Verily I say unto you, There is no man that hath left house, or parents, or brethren, or wife, or children, for the kingdom of God's sake, Who shall not receive

manifold more in this present time, and in the world to come life everlasting. (Luke 18:29–30 KJV)

The apostle Paul declares that the Kingdom benefits are numerous:

> Not because I desire a gift: but I desire fruit that may abound to your account. But I have all, and abound: I am full, having received of Epaphroditus the things which were sent from you, an odour of a sweet smell, a sacrifice acceptable, wellpleasing to God. But my God shall supply all your need according to his riches in glory by Christ Jesus. Now unto God and our Father be glory for ever and ever, Amen. (Philippians 4:17–20 KJV)

> **The King provides all of the ambassador's economic and personal needs while representing the King in another country.**

CHAPTER

Learning to Stay Reconciled

Be ye reconciled to God.

To understand the meaning of "Be ye reconciled," imagine two friends who had an altercation. Afterward the good relationship they once enjoyed is severed to the point of breaking. They no longer are communicating with each other; communication becomes too awkward. Their friendship becomes estranged. Such estrangement can only be reversed by reconciliation. To be reconciled is to be restored to friendship or harmony. When old friends resolve their differences and restore their relationship, reconciliation has occurred. Second Corinthians 5:18–19 declares,

> All this is from God, who reconciled us to himself through Christ and gave us

the ministry of reconciliation: that God was reconciling the world to himself in Christ, not counting men's sins against them. And he has committed to us the message of reconciliation.

The Bible says that Christ reconciled us to God (Romans 5:10, 2 Corinthians 5:18, Colossians 1:20–21). The fact that we needed reconciliation means that our relationship with God was broken. Since God is holy, we were the ones to blame. Our sin alienated us from Him. Romans 5:10 says that we were enemies of God:

> For if, when we were God's enemies, we were reconciled to him through the death of his Son, how much more, having been reconciled, shall we be saved through his life!

The power to remain restored in Christ Jesus is my choice.

When Christ died on the cross, he satisfied God's judgment and made it possible for God's enemies, us, to find peace with Him. Our "reconciliation" to God, then, involves the exercise of His grace and the forgiveness of our sin. The result of Jesus' sacrifice is that our relationship has changed from enmity to friendship.

> I no longer call you servants . . . Instead, I have called you friends. (John 15:15)

Christian reconciliation is a glorious truth! We were God's enemies, but are now His friends. We were in a state of condemnation because of our sins, but we are now forgiven. We were at war with God, but now have the peace that transcends all understanding (Philippians 4:7). Now it is our assignment in this relationship to keep this relationship reconciled.

Staying in Christ is the choice of the new believer, necessary to keep the relationship reconciled, but it is a learned portion of our walk. Apostle John reminds us,

> As many as received him, to them gave he power to become the sons of God, even to them that believe on his name. (John 1:11–12 KJV)

The power that Jesus has given us is the power to yield our minds to the Holy Spirit. Yielding to the Holy Spirit is the believer's personal responsibility to exercise so that we might remain reconciled; this choice is the believer's authority to make. This is the personal power every believer has within his life. Paul declares,

> I live yet not I, but Christ liveth in me: and the life which I now live in the flesh I live by the faith of the Son of God, who loved me, and gave himself for me. (Galatians 2:20 KJV)

We surrender ourselves to the Spirit within us, allowing Christ to live and perform his will to do of his good pleasure within us.

> My beloved, as ye have always obeyed, not as in my presence only, but now much more in my absence, work out your own salvation with fear and trembling. For it is God which worketh in you both to will and to do of his good pleasure. Do all things without murmurings and disputings: That ye may be blameless and harmless, the sons of God, without rebuke, in the midst of a crooked and perverse nation, among

I refuse to surrender the power of Kingdom Thinking

whom ye shine as lights in the world. (Philippians 2:12–15 KJV)

Again apostle Paul reinforces this thought by saying,

> What the law could not do, in that it was weak through the flesh, God sending his own Son in the likeness of sinful flesh, and for sin, condemned sin in the flesh: That the righteousness of the law might be fulfilled in us, who walk not after the flesh, but after the Spirit. For they that are after the flesh do mind the things of the flesh; but they that are after the Spirit the things of the Spirit. (Romans 8:3–5 KJV)

So we are those who walk after the Spirit and not the flesh.

> They that are Christ's have crucified the flesh with the affections and lusts. If we live in the Spirit, let us also walk in the Spirit. (Galatians 5:24–25 KJV)

This is how we remain reconciled to God. When we are challenged with sin in our daily walk with Christ, we must understand that we are learning how to walk by the Spirit within us. There will be times that we will sometimes fall. Jesus understands that, and Paul addresses this matter also:

> What shall we say then? Shall we continue in sin when we fall that grace may abound? God forbid. How shall we, that are dead to sin, live any longer therein? (Romans 6:1–2 KJV)

We are not to live in sin any longer, yet there will be times when one falls in sin. Paul says that you should know this by now!

> Know ye not, that so many of us as were baptized [the Holy Ghost] into Jesus Christ were baptized [the Spirit of Christ] into his death? Therefore we are buried with him by baptism into death: that like as Christ was raised up from the dead by the glory of the Father, even so we also should walk in newness of life. For if we have been planted together in the likeness of his death, we shall be also in the likeness of his resurrection: Knowing this, that our old man is crucified with him, that the body [flesh] of sin might be

destroyed, that henceforth we should not serve sin. For he that is dead is freed from sin. (Romans 6:3–7 KJV)

Whenever believers find themselves in sin they repent, ask the Lord to forgive them, then allow the Spirit to get them back on track by walking with the Spirit, remembering,

> **The Spirit of God leads us but we make the choice.**

There is now no condemnation to them which are in Christ Jesus, who walk not after the flesh, but after the Spirit. For the law of the Spirit of life in Christ Jesus hath made me free from the law of sin and death. (Romans 8:1–2 KJV)

Yes, when we sin we have learned how to confess our sins immediately.

If we say that we have no sin, we deceive ourselves, and the truth is not in us. If we confess our sins, he is faithful and just to forgive us our sins, and to cleanse us from all unrighteousness. If we say that we have not sinned, we make him a liar, and his word is not in us. (1 John 1:8–10 KJV)

This is another reason that the Spirit is necessary, it cleans us of all sin when we confess our sins.

> How much more shall the blood of Christ, who through the eternal Spirit offered himself without spot to God, purge your conscience from dead works to serve the living God? (Hebrews 9:14 KJV)

That is awesome: that the cleansing, restoring power of the blood of Jesus is within you by the Spirit of Christ, and that it will wash you clean of all sins if you confess. We are learning how to put away everything that trips us up in our walk.

> Wherefore seeing we also are compassed about with so great a cloud of witnesses, let us lay aside every weight, and the sin which doth so easily beset us, and let us run with patience the race that is set before us, Looking unto Jesus the author and finisher of our faith; who for the joy that was set before him endured the cross, despising the shame, and is set down at the right hand of the throne of God. (Hebrews 12:1–2 KJV)

This is how we stay in the will of Christ and remain reconciled to God.

This is the story we share with friends and loved ones who don't understand this Christian walk and think that we have it all together. We are in Christ and what they see is the Christ that lives in us. This is a faith walk and without faith in Him we cannot please God.

> *He hath made him to be sin for us,*
> *who knew no sin.*

CHAPTER

We Are Christ's Workmanship

... that we might be made the righteousness of God in him.

The Apostle Paul understood that his Kingdom assignment was to build the body of Christ that he once destroyed. This is also why the Lord can tremendously use your previous life in sin to build the present Kingdom of God. This is the entry-level of ministry known as the ambassadors. This is your "you can get busy for Jesus right now" ministry, the *only* requirements are found in 2 Corinthian 5:17. The book was written to help readers understand their entry-level calling. This is the power and authority that they have been given by receiving the promise of the Father, and their assignment on the earth is to preach the gospel.

Children of God, these are the divine God-given credentials to every new believer. To not understand this, which is the value of your calling to your Savior, is inexcusable.

> Ignorance of this is blasphemous and a trick of the demonic forces on the earth called the prince of the power of the air. (Ephesians 2:2)

The apostle Paul writings are the writings to the first church, the new believers. These writings are not to the unregenerate man; these letters are to those who have been redeemed by the blood of the lamb. These letters also give in detail the administrative structures to the body of Christ.

> Those who are reconciled to God have power to continue to surrender themselves to Christ and remain reconciled.

Welcome! So, you have given your life to Jesus? You believe in Jesus! You have faith in God? That means that you have repented from your past sins and have decided to walk by faith with Jesus? You have also been baptized in Jesus' name? Just checking to make sure that we are on the same page. Just checking to make sure that you have followed these necessary steps to qualify you for the entry-level credentials, along with the benefits promised to all the family members of the Kingdom of God.

www.ingramcontent.com/pod-product-compliance
Lightning Source LLC
Chambersburg PA
CBHW021130300426
44113CB00006B/369